DIE STORIE VAN GETALLE

THE NUMBER STORY

SMALL BOOK ONE

ENGLISH - AFRICAANS

Numbers Teach Children
Their Number Names

written and illustrated by

MISS ANNA

Early Reader Edition of *The Number Story 1*
Bronze Medal Winner, 2016 Wishing Shelf Book Award

Library of Congress Control Number: 2018902040

Names: Miss Anna, author.
Title: Number story : numbers teach children their number names / Miss Anna.
Description: Portland, OR: Lumpy Publishing, 2018.
Identifiers: ISBN 978-1-945977-77-0| LCCN 2018902040
Summary: The pictures and rhymes present stories which introduce numbers 0-10.
Subjects: LCSH Numeration—English--Africaans--Pictorial works--Juvenile literature. | BISAC JUVENILE NONFICTION /
Languages: English--Africaans
Classification: LCC QA141.3 .M57 2018 | DDC 513—dc23

Publisher: Lumpy Publishing
Website: www.missannabooks.com
Email: missanna@missannabooks.com

Paperback: ISBN 978-1-945977-77-0
Printed in the U.S.A.   1 3 5 7 9 10 8 6 4 2

Wil jy die name
van getalle leer?

It is very easy and a lot of fun!

Dit is baie maklik en 'n klomp pret!

Say-along our little jingle

Sing ons klein storie saam met ons!

starting from Number One!

Kom ons begin by nommer een!

1

ONE   looks like my one finger.

EEN

lyk soos my een finger.

ONE!
EEN!

2

TWO   trails a tail.

TWEE

sleep 'n stert.

A TAIL! 'N STERT!

3

THREE has bumps.

DRIE

het kurwes.

Kyk na die kurwes!

4
FOUR carries a sail.
VIER
het 'n seil.

4
A SAIL!
'N boot
met 'n seil!

5

FIVE   is a racing track.

VYF

is n ren baan.

VROOM
VROEM!

6

S I X   curves like a snail.

SES

krul soos 'n slak.

A SNAIL!   'N SLAK!

7

SEVEN has a sharp angle.

SEWE

het n skerp hoek.

BE CAREFUL! IT'S SHARP!

Wees versigtig! Dit is skerp!

8

EIGHT   is rollercoaster rails.

AGT

is 'n wipwaentjie.

JIPPIEEE!
YIPPEE!

9

NINE   is a bubble on a stick.

NEGE

is 'n borrel op 'n stok.

A BUBBLE! 'N BORREL!

10

TEN   is an eye of a whale.

TIEN

is een oog van 'n walvis.

KNIPOOG!
WINK!
HELLO! HALLO!

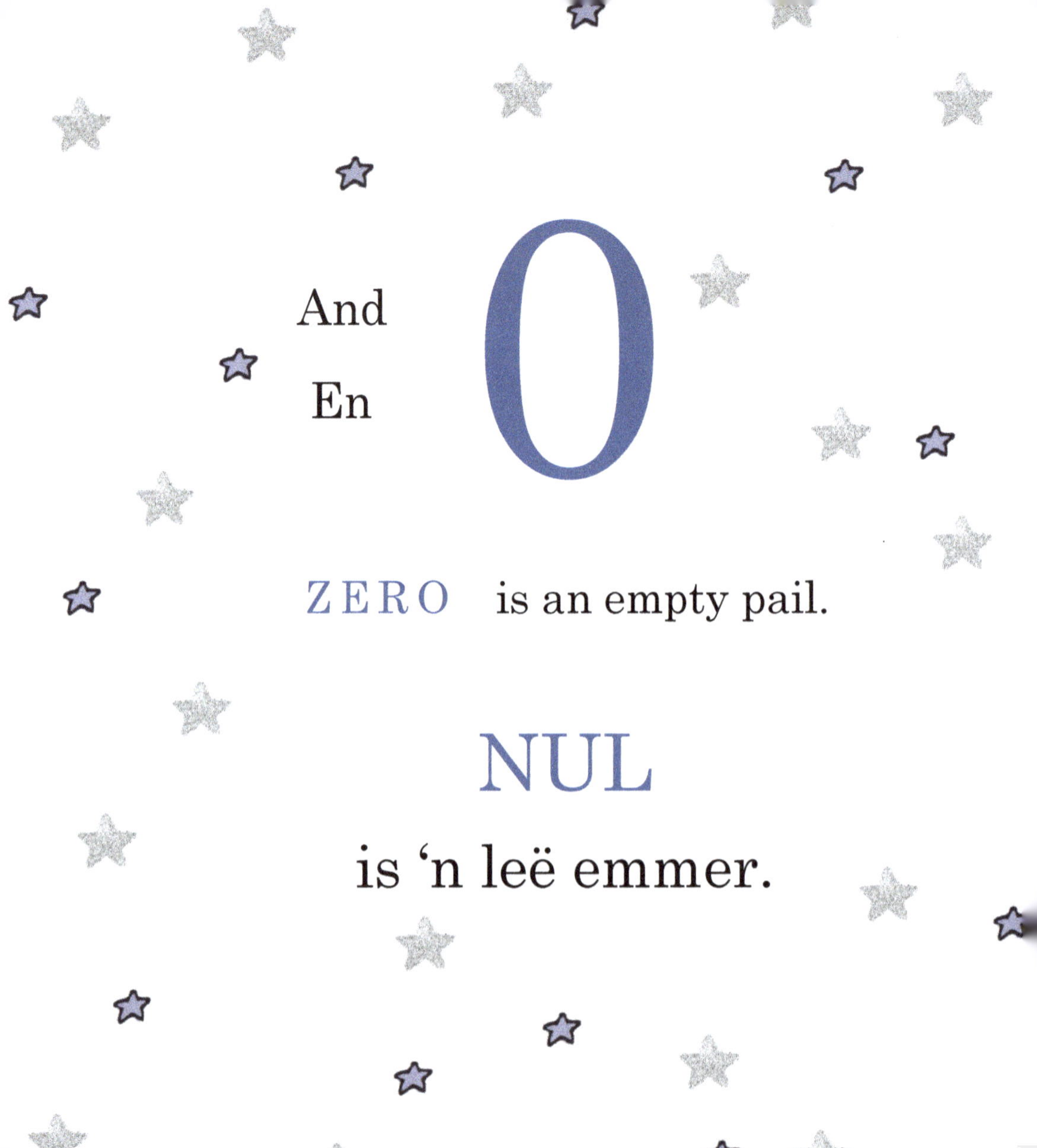

And

En

0

ZERO is an empty pail.

NUL

is 'n leë emmer.

IT'S
EMPTY!

Dit is leeg!

Thank you for playing with us today.

We had a lot of fun too!

Dankie dat jy vandag saam
met ons gespeel het.
Ons het ook 'n klomp pret gehad!

We are your Number friends,
Zero to Ten,
Who will be here for you~

Ons is jou nommer vriende
Nul tot Tien.
Ons sal altyd hier wees vir jou.

Bye-bye now!
See you again soon!

Totsiens vir nou!
Sien jou gou weer!

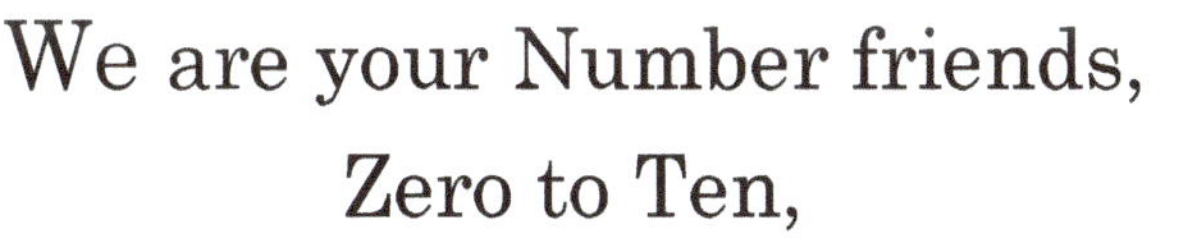

The Numbers are *SINGING* too!

To sing-a-long, look for Miss Anna Number Story
at your favorite music store like iTUNES.

Numbers 0-10
IDENTIFYING
& COUNTING

Numbers 11-20
& Ordinals
first, second, third...

Numbers 0-100
& Place Values
ones, tens, hundreds...

About Cloc
& Telling T
hours, minutes, se

Number Story 1 & 2
isbn: 978-0-996216-48-7

Number Story 3 & 4
isbn: 978-1-945977-01-5

Number Story 5 & 6
isbn: 978-1-945977-06-0

Number Story 7
isbn: 978-1-94932(

For more Miss Anna books to love,
visit us at

www.missannabooks.com

Numbers are working hard all over the world!
Come Travel the World with Us!

www.ingramcontent.com/pod-product-compliance
Lightning Source LLC
Chambersburg PA
CBHW041059050726
47599CB00018B/2203